THE CHANGING
FACE
OF MAPS

Tim Cooke

Crabtree Publishing Company
www.crabtreebooks.com

Crabtree Publishing Company

www.crabtreebooks.com

1-800-387-7650

Published in Canada
616 Welland Ave.
St. Catharines, ON
L2M 5V6

Published in the United States
PMB 59051
350 Fifth Ave. 59th Floor
New York, NY 10118

Published in 2017 by CRABTREE PUBLISHING COMPANY

Author: Tim Cooke

Designer: Melissa Roskell

Cover Design: Katherine Berti

Picture Manager: Sophie Mortimer

Design Manager: Keith Davis

Editorial Director: Lindsey Lowe, Kathy Middleton

Editor: Janine Deschenes

Children's Publisher: Anne O'Daly

Proofreader: Ellen Rodger

Production coordinator and Prepress technician: Ken Wright

Print coordinator: Margaret Amy Salter

Produced by Brown Bear Books for Crabtree Publishing Company

Photo credits

Photographs (t=top, b=bottom, l=left, r=right, c=center)

Front Cover: All images from Shutterstock

Interior: 123RF: scanrail 25; Alamy: The Print Collector 23br; Facebook: 8/9b; Google Earth: 26t, 29t; Human Connectome Project: 5tr; Jan Ulrich Kossemann: 18; Library of Congress: 8/9t, 12, 15b; MTA/NYCT: 28cr; NASA: 6/7, 6bl, 11, 21; NASA: Hubble 26/27; National Maritime Museum: 24tr; Natural Enquirer: Benjamin Hennig 7; New York Port Authority: 29br; notonthehighstreet.com: alice.tate 28bl; Robert Hunt Library: 14/15, 16, 17t, 18/19b, 20, 23tr; Science Photo Library: 22/23; Shutterstock: Andrey Armyagov 27tr, Garsya 24br, Marzolino 4, 10; The New York Pass: 29bl; Thinkstock: Photos.com 5bl; U.S. Army: 13. All other photos, artwork and maps, Brown Bear Books.

Brown Bear Books has made every attempt to contact the copyright holder. If you have any information please contact licensing@brownbearbooks.co.uk

Library and Archives Canada Cataloguing in Publication

Cooke, Tim, 1961-, author
      The changing face of maps / Tim Cooke.

(Mapping in the modern world)
Includes index.
Issued in print and electronic formats.
ISBN 978-0-7787-3221-1 (hardcover).--
ISBN 978-0-7787-3239-6 (softcover).--
ISBN 978-1-4271-1882-0 (HTML)

        1. Cartography--Juvenile literature. 2. Maps--Juvenile
literature. 3. Cartography--History--Juvenile literature. 4.
Cartography--Technological innovations--Juvenile literature. I. Title.

GA105.6.C66 2017   j526   C2016-907113-8
                                                         C2016-907114-6

Library of Congress Cataloging-in-Publication Data

CIP available at the Library of Congress

Printed in Canada/052017/TL20170327

Contents

WHAT IS A MAP?

There are many different types of map. Although we often associate maps with images drawn on paper, modern maps cover a range of different purposes and **media**.

It is easier to recognize a map than to describe what a map is. Traditional maps are two-dimensional drawings of a place used for **navigation** or for establishing boundaries between land owned by different people. Other maps represent information rather than geography. The information might be **concrete**, such as the size of a population, or **abstract**, such as average wealth. Many modern maps are actually photographs, while some maps deliberately distort, or change, the shape and size of geographical regions.

This map of North America was created by Louis Hennepin, a priest and explorer, in 1698. At this time **cartographers** left unexplored regions blank.

New Definitions

Cartography, the study of maps, has evolved over time. Today, most cartographers see maps as graphic representations not only of places but also of events, conditions, or even ideas. This definition includes images that would not have traditionally been considered as maps, such as diagrams of the human body. For example, the Human Connectome Project is an ambitious program that aims to track the workings of the brain as a series of maps. Researchers hope to map the billions of pathways in the human brain to better understand how our **nervous system** is connected.

Using special devices, researchers for the Human Connectome Project create maps such as the one above, which shows different color-coded pathways in the brain.

New Media

New definitions of maps have to include a wider range of technology and media. Some modern maps are on screens rather than on paper. They use technology that changes the map to follow the user's surroundings. Smartphone apps allow users to track their own routes on **Geographic Information Systems** (GIS). Unlike traditional maps, these maps are tailored to a person and his or her surroundings. They can plot the best route between two places and follow progress along it. They can even show how long the journey will take.

Mapping apps on smartphones are customized to their users' needs and preferences.

Images from Space

Some modern maps are based on images of Earth taken from space. In 1972, the Earth Resources Technology **Satellite** was launched. It was later renamed Landsat. Since then, Landsat satellites have orbited Earth, taking photographs of the planet's surface. The satellites do not only photograph changes in the visual appearance of the land, however. They use **thermal imaging** and **radar** to "photograph" things that are not visible on Earth, such as the temperature of the oceans and changing sea levels.

One of the most ambitious modern mapping projects is Google Earth. Launched in 2005, it aims to allow computer users to view Earth's surface in three dimensions, or 3D.

Did You Know?

The images on Google Earth appear to be regular satellite photographs. In fact, they are made up of many different images with images taken from airplanes and ground-based observations.

2012

2000

These images from the Landsat satellite show the same part of the Amazon rain forest in Brazil at different times. Forest areas are dark green, while logged areas are lighter green and brown. The straight lines are roads.

Breakthroughs

Tracking Resources

The Landsat program is just one way for mapmakers to monitor natural resources. The United States Geological Survey has launched a project to record details of landform, soil, and land cover in a vast database. The survey divides Earth's surface into 820-foot (250-meter) square cells called Ecological Land Units. It gathers information for each cell. The information is used to generate layers of color-coding that can be used on maps. The layers can be combined into highly detailed maps of resources such as trees, fresh water, or rocks and minerals.

Presenting Data

Some cartographers are not interested in reflecting the physical qualities of the world. In a form of map known as a **cartogram**, areas are deliberately distorted. Cartograms use maps to show comparisons between different parts of a community, country, or of the whole world. Cartograms are a striking way to show **statistical** information that is converted into maps by computer programs.

This cartogram shows the expected population in 2050. China and India are largest, because they will have the largest populations. The colors help indicate the countries in each continent.

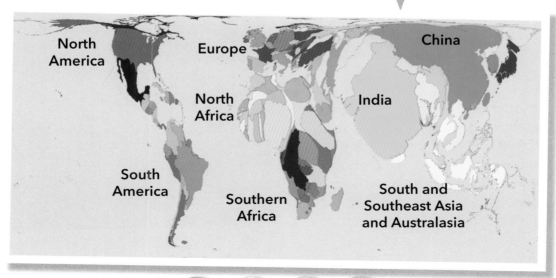

Read This Map

This map was drawn in the 1980s. It shows the zoo in Washington, D.C. **Keys** on the bottom right and left sides help viewers understand the symbols and colors on the map. What are the most obvious features when you first look at the map? What has the mapmaker left out? Do you think it would be useful to visitors as they navigate around the zoo? Why? Are there any problems with this type of map?

Geographic Information Systems (GIS)

Since the 1970s, the growth of computers has changed maps. Computers make it possible to gather and store huge amounts of data. GIS are computer programs that gather data about the climate, terrain, vegetation, soils, and other features of specific locations.

GIS gather information from a wide range of sources, including satellite images and sets of statistics. They turn the data into visual displays that can be shown on maps. The data can range from geographical features and land use to population numbers and average income. The mapmaker chooses which data to include or leave out based on the purpose of the map.

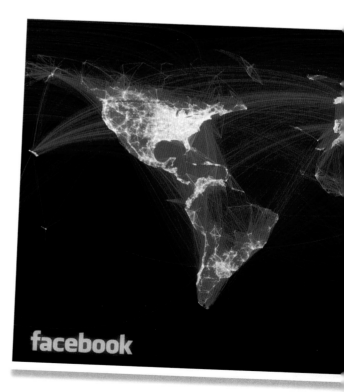

al Park

Olmsted Walk

1 **Information** Education Building, Books, Gifts, Audio Tour Rental, Wheelchairs, Strollers
2 Cheetah Conservation Station
3 Panda Cafe*
4 **Information*** Audio Tour Rental, Strollers, Wheelchairs
5 Pandas, Camels
6 Elephants, Giraffes
7 Hippos, Rhinos
8 American Bison
9 American Indian Heritage Garden
10 Small Mammal House
11 Great Ape House
12 Gibbon Ridge
13 Reptile Discovery Center (controlled access**)
14 Invertebrate Exhibit (controlled access**)
15 Exhibit in Progress
16 Servals, Leopards
17 Lions, Tigers
18 Monkey Island
19 African American Heritage Garden
20 Bears
21 Police
22 Bat Cave
23 Mane Restaurant
24 **Information*** Audio Tour Rental, Strollers, Wheelchairs

This map of the Washington Zoo combines realistic illustration of trees and other details with the bird's-eye view normally used by maps to show features clearly.

Mapping Relationships

Some maps show how things relate to each other rather than distance or place. One example of this is the map of the London Underground, the huge subway system in London, England. The London Underground map was drawn by the engineer Harry Beck in 1933. Beck understood that travelers on the subway only needed to know their destination, the order in which the stations occurred on their journey, and about the intersections between lines.

Many modern maps visualize large **datasets** of information. Cartographers map Twitter messages or the location of Facebook members by gathering data from the Internet. These kinds of maps show the space and form of social interactions that exist online.

This 2010 map shows connections on Facebook. It is an example of mapping relationships rather than things.

Breakthroughs

Origins of Mapmaking

The first maps showed the sky, not the Earth. In around 16,500 B.C.E. an artist in what is now France painted three dots on a cave wall to mark the positions of three bright stars. Around 4,000 years later, an artist in Spain painted another constellation in a cave.

USES OF MAPS

Maps have many different purposes. Some show a range of general information. Others show detailed information about a specific subject.

Throughout history, the most important purposes for maps have fallen into three types. Many maps have been created for navigation, or finding the way; others are used for **surveying**, or defining areas and boundaries; and a third type of map is used to present different types of information.

Navigation Maps

Some maps allow people to plan and follow a route. Navigation maps include road maps for drivers, air and sea charts for pilots and ships'

This sea chart of the Atlantic Ocean was drawn for sailors in the 1500s. It shows Africa and South America, with ports listed on the coasts and bearing lines for navigation.

Navigation in Space

In 1969, when Apollo 11 flew to the Moon, the astronauts took star charts (below). To find their position, they identified three stars and entered the stars' coordinates into a computer. The computer figured out where Apollo was and what course it should take. Apart from the computer, the method was the same as sailors used in the 1600s and 1700s.

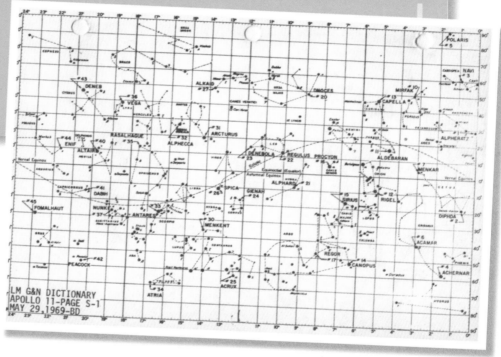

captains, and street maps for people in cities and towns. Early navigation maps were created for sailors. They had lines between ports, or places where ships can dock, to show sailors what **bearing**, or direction, to follow. A **compass rose** showed which way the map should be **oriented**. European seafarers such as Christopher Columbus explored much of the world from the 1400s to the 1700s. They mapped their voyages in Asia, the Americas, and the Pacific Ocean so that later explorers could retrace their routes.

The Apollo charts grouped stars into constellations. These patterns are a useful guide to help identify stars. At different times, people have seen different shapes, or constellations, among the stars.

This strip map of the road from New York to La Rochelle was drawn in 1789. It shows three sections of the same road.

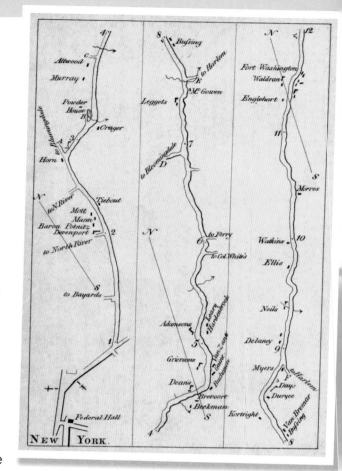

Strip Maps

Some navigation maps exclude any information that does not directly affect a traveler. Strip maps do not indicate bends in the road. Instead, they show routes as a straight line and highlight the location of towns and the distance between them. They are only useful if someone is making the specific journey they illustrate.

Survey Maps

Some maps are used to define particular areas of land. These maps might record who owns what real estate, while survey maps might define where one community ends and another begins, or even where one country borders another.

Maps that record the borders between and locations of different countries, states, cities, counties, and other communities are called political maps. Political maps record the boundaries that governments make. Boundaries are often subject to fierce disputes. Surveyors and cartographers work out precisely what route a boundary follows, so that the map reflects the reality.

In the Real World

The Length of the Border

Maps drawn in Spain often show Spain's border with Portugal as being far shorter than maps drawn in Portugal. This might reflect the fact that Portuguese cartographers concentrate more on tracing tiny changes in the border more accurately. Portugal is only about a quarter of the size of Spain, so these small differences are more important to Portuguese cartographers.

Information Maps

Maps are useful for presenting information that is related to space or area. This might be population size or the availability of rental bikes in a city. Common types of information maps include topographical maps, and geological maps. Topographical maps show geographical features such as mountains and rivers. Geological maps show the formation of rocks beneath the ground. Other types of maps include historical maps, which show

This 1944 map uses colors to show the changing course of the Mississippi River in the past. It is an example of an historical map.

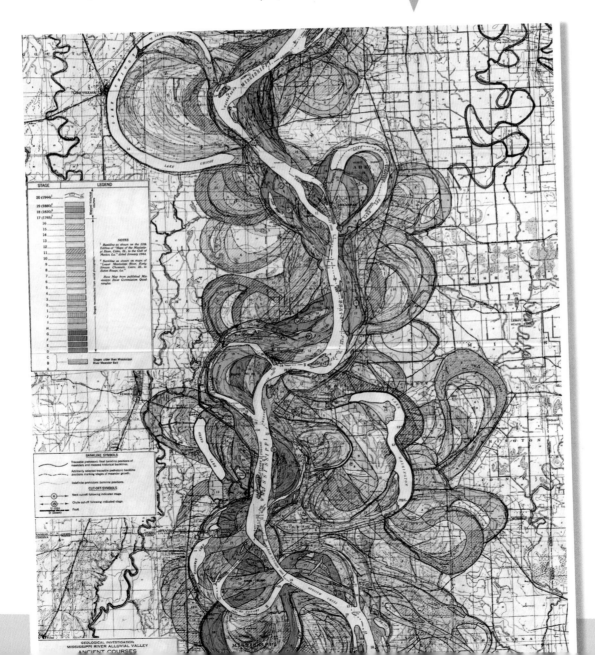

A Smaller Country

In 1682, experts at the Academy of Sciences in Paris revised old maps of France. They used scientific methods to measure the country's coastline accurately. They realized that previous maps were wrong. They moved the Atlantic coast 1.5 degrees east and the Mediterranean coast 0.5 degrees north. In one blow, the area of France had been reduced by several hundred square miles.

places as they were, and ecological maps, which show where different types of wildlife and plants live. Information on such maps is presented through color coding or a key, through symbols, or through writing out facts. Information can also be displayed in more graphic ways, such as in a cartogram.

The revised coastline (dark line) is quite a lot farther west than on previous maps.

Cosmological Maps

Maps that show the universe in a way that reflects religious teachings are called **cosmological** maps. In early maps created by followers of Hindu, Buddhist, and Jain religions, the universe is arranged in a series of **concentric** circles around a central mountain. Cosmological maps are linked to maps of stars and other **astronomical** bodies, such as planets. For centuries, the position of astronomical bodies in the sky was used for navigation. The regular movements of these bodies were also used to figure out the calendar of the seasons.

Did You Know?

Medieval Christian cosmological maps were called T-O maps. They showed the earth as a round "O" divided into three by a T shape. The three continents known in the Middle Ages were Europe, Asia, and Africa.

Recording Other Realities

Some maps do not represent only things that physically exist. Mind maps or word maps try to record ideas and the relationships between them. Many artists use maps in creative ways, such as drawing imaginary places. Other maps are used as **propaganda**, which means that they may present misleading or inaccurate information to make people think a certain way. An example of this are late-19th-century maps produced by towns in the Midwest United States to attract settlers. These maps were often drawn as a bird's-eye view, which combined a map with a painting. The maps showed thriving towns, but when the settlers arrived they often found that the "town" was only a few cabins along a road or river.

This bird's-eye map shows Chattanooga, Tennessee, in 1871. The map shows the ambitious layout of the streets, but at the time there were few actual buildings.

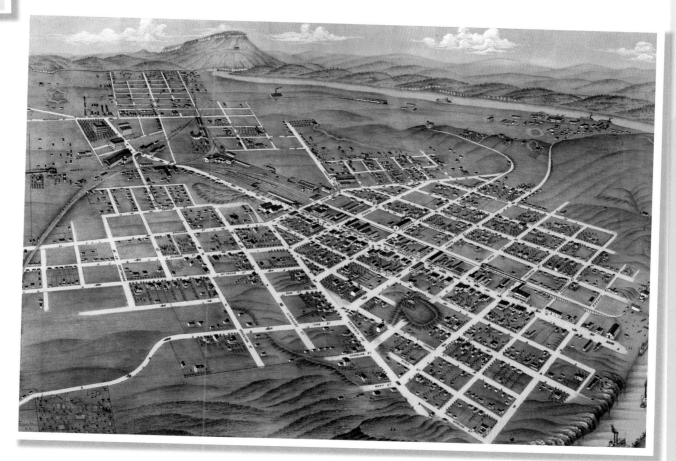

HISTORY OF MAPS

People have been making maps for almost as long as they have been able to paint or draw. Maps have always played a key role in the development of human history.

Maps are some of the oldest of all historical documents. People drew what may be maps long before writing was invented. In France, people mapped the stars on the walls of the Lascaux Cave in 16,500 B.C.E. An early map found in Italy showed the fields attached to one village. The people who invented writing (the Sumerians who lived in Mesopotamia in c.3200 B.C.E.) drew maps on clay **tablets**. In ancient Egypt, meanwhile, maps drawn on a fabric called linen showed the way to stone quarries, or large pits, in the desert.

This map was based on the **projection** figured out by the Greek-Egyptian Claudius Ptolemy in about 150 C.E. The faces represent the major winds.

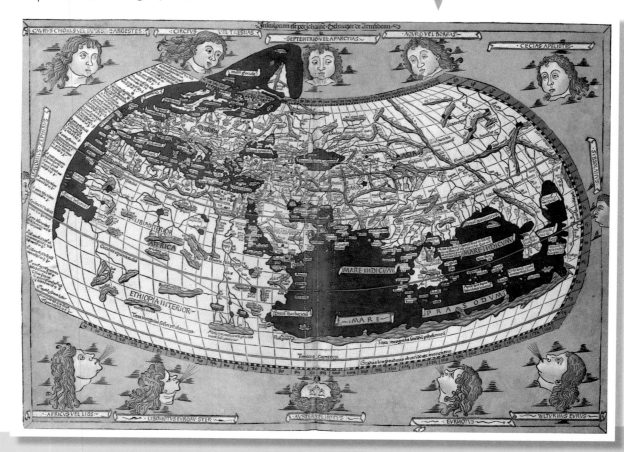

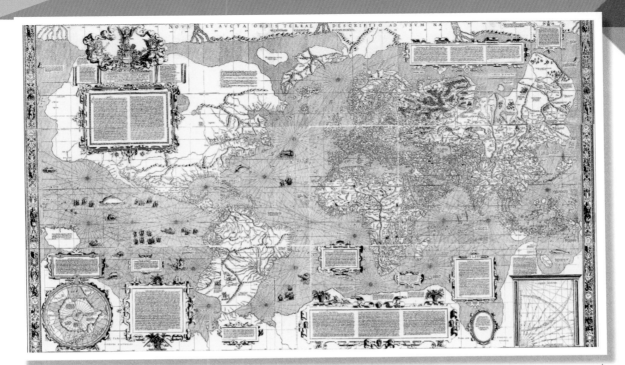

In ancient Greece and Rome, maps were used by governments. They allowed land to be distributed to retired soldiers in return for their service, or were used to value land for **taxation**.

New Projections

In the second century C.E., a Greek-Egyptian geographer named Claudius Ptolemy began to consider one of the key problems facing mapmakers. How can mapmakers show the three-dimensional surface of Earth on a two-dimensional map? Flattening Earth's surface to make it two dimensional involves distorting it in some way, a process called projection. Ptolemy's answer was to divide maps by a grid of lines of latitude (running north–south) and longitude (running east–west). The grid helped show where distortion had taken place.

Ptolemy is often seen as the first true cartographer because of his emphasis on mathematical accuracy. Since his time, many other geographers have come up with ways to project a map onto a flat piece of paper with minimal distortion.

Mercator drew his map in 1569. Experts still do not know how he figured out the math needed to create his projection.

Breakthroughs

Map Projections

The way in which the globe is shown on a flat map is called a projection. There have been many types of projection. They all distort the shape of the world to some degree. The best known is the Mercator projection. It shows Greenland as far bigger than it actually is, but Africa and Latin America are relatively small. Mercator drew them this way because it helped sailors plot more accurate courses at sea.

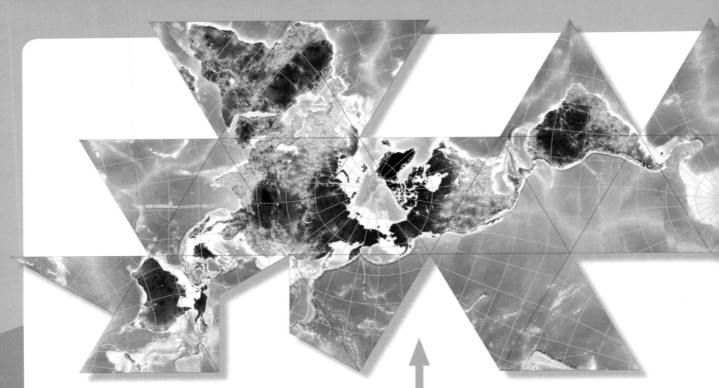

Today it is possible to make three-dimensional maps of Earth. This map is based on a multi-sided shape, or polyhedron. The map could be cut out and folded to make a 3D model of the world.

In the 1940s, the U.S. architect Richard Buckminster Fuller created a "dymaxion" world map. The design projects Earth's surface onto a 20-faced polyhedron, then flattens the faces out. The most common **geometric** projection still in use was invented by the Flemish cartographer Gerardus Mercator in 1569.

The Religious View

Not all mapmakers followed Ptolemy's ambition to create accurate maps of Earth. In the Middle Ages, like today, there were many different types of maps. Christian maps continued to show the universe as it was described in the Bible, even after geographical discoveries made it clear that they were not accurate depictions of Earth.

Buddhist, Hindu, and Jain cartographers also set out to depict a universe based on **scripture** rather than observation of the world. Other maps set out accurate paths for **pilgrims** to follow to religious sites. Experts think that some of these maps were only ever intended to help people make imaginary journeys.

Discovering the World

The earliest sailing charts appeared around 1250. Called portolan charts, these were used by sailors in the Atlantic Ocean and Mediterranean Sea. They listed the names of ports around a coast, together with compass directions. There were no inland features. From the portolans emerged the maps of the Age of Discovery. This was a period from roughly the 1400s to the 1600s when European seafarers made long voyages to parts of the world they had not visited before. What they discovered in Africa, Asia, the Americas, and the Pacific was recorded in increasingly scientific maps.

This map of the Americas was drawn in Holland in the 1600s, when Dutch ships were sailing around the world for trade.

Map Symbols

Over time, some map symbols have become standard. Blue lines indicate rivers, for example. The height of the land, or relief, is often shown by contour lines. These lines link places that are the same height above sea level. Contour lines packed closely together indicate very steep slopes.

Breakthroughs

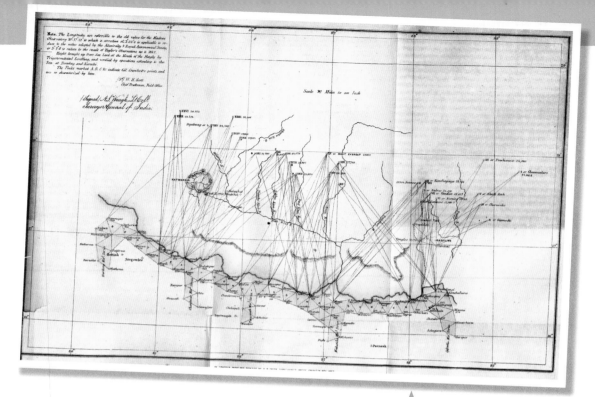

The Age of Discovery happened at the same time as the Scientific Revolution. During this time, discoveries in math and astronomy, all helped produce more accurate maps. Some experts believe the increasing accuracy of maps had an influence on the creation of modern countries, because maps helped define their borders.

This map of northern India was drawn by British surveyors in the 1800s. Accurate maps were drawn to help Britain's colonial government of India.

Mapping and Colonies

From the 1600s to the 1800s, mapping expeditions helped record previously unknown areas as Europeans started **colonies** in Africa and Asia, and as settlement spread west across America. Mapping became a key part of government, and surveyors mapped many remote regions.

Maps were usually compiled by **Western** cartographers. Since the maps were mostly drawn from their perspectives, they did not include information such as the loose boundaries between the territories of **Indigenous** nations. Because of this, new borders often split up Indigenous communities.

Did You Know?

U.S. Army engineers were the first people to map the American West in the late 1800s. The surveyors of the Corps of Topographical Engineers helped to find routes for the building of the transcontinental railroads.

By the 1900s, maps were everywhere. Children learned about the world from maps in classrooms. The public followed the course of World War I (1914 to 1918) and World War II (1939 to 1945) on maps in newspapers. As car ownership increased between the wars, motorists began following road maps that were often handed out free by oil companies. From the 1950s, viewers became used to seeing weather maps on their TVs.

Mapping Goes into Space

The late 1900s introduced changes to maps and how people use them. In 1957, the Soviet Union launched the first satellite into orbit around Earth. As more satellites were launched, they gave cartographers unparalleled information about the Earth. The rise of computers and the Internet gave people access to **digital** mapping displayed on screens. Together, satellite and computer technology formed the basis of the Global Positioning System (GPS), which allows users to access maps of their precise location.

The Gall-Peters Projection is an example of an equal-area map. A unit of area in one continent matches exactly with the same unit of area in another continent.

Maps and Me

Read This Map

This map is based on a projection invented by Arno Peters in 1973.

Peters' map had been based on a map that was drawn by James Gall in 1855. Peters was an historian rather than a mapmaker. He thought that most maps put too much emphasis on the Northern Hemisphere. Peters wanted to show the relative sizes of the regions of the world. Compare it with the Mercator projection on pages 18 to 19. What advantages can you see in using the Gall-Peters Projection?

MAPS AND TECHNOLOGY

People have always used new technology to create maps. Meanwhile, the desire to make better records of the world has spurred the development of new forms of technology.

Cartographers in the past led many developments in math as well as technology. The ancient Greeks knew that Earth was round. A mathematician named Eratosthenes estimated its **diameter**. His calculation was remarkably accurate. He was only off by 15 percent. The Greeks also devised a grid of lines across maps. This helped to display a **spherical** planet on a flat surface by showing where distortions occurred. These lines were the basis of the system of latitude and longitude still used today.

Did You Know?

Triangulation is a mathematical technique. It uses the angles and measurements of two sides of a triangle to figure out the length of the third side.

This drawing from the 1600s shows a sailor using a telescope to study the stars to figure out his location.

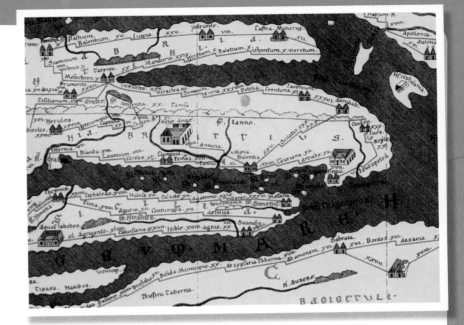

This map from the 1200s is a recreation of a map drawn in Rome around the year 0 c.e. It shows Roman roads (red) in Italy (top), Sicily (middle), and North Africa (bottom).

In ancient Greece and Rome, measurements for maps were taken by surveyors. A surveyor is a person who examines or assesses land. A technique known as triangulation helped surveyors figure out distances. Triangulation used the distance of two known points to calculate the distance of a third. The technique—the basis of early mapping—remained at the heart of mapping for centuries.

In this drawing, a surveyor uses a quadrant to measure the height of a church tower using triangulation.

New Technology

In the Middle Ages, technological developments made maps more accurate. Devices such as the **sextant** and the **astrolabe** allowed navigators to measure their location relative to the position of objects in space. Navigators used this information to draw charts as they sailed to new parts of the world.

This marine chronometer was invented by John Harrison in 1761. It kept time accurately even on long sea voyages.

Increasing Accuracy

On early maps, any direction could be at the top. In the 1400s, however, it became common to show north at the top. In the 1760s, sailors became able to figure out accurately their longitude, or east–west position on the globe. This relied on knowing the difference in time between their location and the time where they had begun their journey. The invention of a chronometer, or clock, that kept accurate time at sea made this possible.

Later, exploration encouraged the development of new methods of surveying that resulted in more accurate maps. In the 1800s this included the Great Trigonometrical Survey, carried out by Britain to map its colony in India. In the United States, military engineers mapped the West in order to establish railroad routes.

A compass shows magnetic north rather than true north. The variation between the two points is different in different locations on the Earth's surface.

Magnetic North

When a compass points north, it points to the magnetic North Pole. That is the top of Earth's magnetic field. However, magnetic north is not the same as the geographic North Pole, which is the northernmost point on the planet. The difference between the two in degrees is called magnetic declination. The variation changes by 1 or 2 degrees every century. This can make old maps unreliable.

After the invention of the airplane in 1903, aerial photography was used in World War I (1914 to 1918). After the war, aerial photography became widespread. Photographs of towns and cities or wider regions allowed increased accuracy in the drawing of maps. The first "hybrid" maps appeared that combined photographs with map features such as labels or a key.

Influence of Computers

Advances in technology continued to influence mapmaking. Advances in computing in the 1950s led in the 1970s to the development of **computational geometry** and **spatial analysis**. Computerized Geographic Information Systems (GIS) were developed to gather huge amounts of information and convert it so it can be displayed on maps.

For most of history, maps were printed on paper. The maps were engraved on stone or metal, covered with ink, and pressed on to paper. Today many maps are displayed digitally on screens. They can be static, like paper maps, but they can also be dynamic or interactive. Digital maps can be continuously updated to display information in real time.

Modern route planners are most often used on tablets and cell phones that can continuously redraw a map as the user moves around.

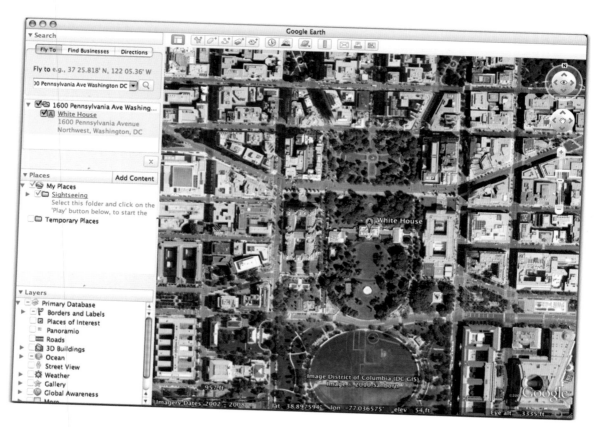

Satellite Mapping

The launch of earth-orbiting satellites has made it possible to "map" Earth continuously. The Landsat program that began in 1972 records not only the visible surface, but also qualities such as ground temperature. Satellite technology also lies behind the Global Positioning System (GPS). This enables users to create customized maps that pinpoint their location and map a route to a destination.

The Google Earth project began in 2005. It aims to compile satellite maps of all parts of Earth. The maps include elements such as labels for streets, buildings, and geographical features. Users can zoom in and out to achieve higher levels of detail. In some cities, the highest **resolution** shows details that may be only 6 inches (15 cm) across.

This Google Earth image shows the White House in Washington, D.C. The side menu shows different features, such as places of interest, the user can include in a map.

In the Real World

Measuring Location

For centuries, people have used the regular movement of the planets and stars to figure out their location on Earth. Some of the earliest geographical devices were made to measure the height of such heavenly bodies above the horizon. The astrolabe was a more complex version of these simple devices. Today, modern GPS technology also uses the position of objects in space to triangulate locations on Earth. GPS technology uses artificial computerized satellites in space, instead of stars and planets, to figure out locations.

Mapping Space

Some of the most recent technology is being used to map the universe. In 2016 the European Space Agency space observatory Gaia began mapping a billion stars. It will eventually produce the most accurate map of the universe ever created.

There are more than 2,200 satellites in orbit above Earth. Of those, around 24 are part of the GPS system.

This photograph of a distant galaxy was taken by the Hubble Space Telescope. Images like these allow astronomers to map the far parts of the universe.

MAPS IN YOUR WORLD

A cartographer always has to make choices about what to show on a map and what to leave out. The results can be very different, depending on the map's purpose.

Look at the maps on these pages. They are all different but they all show the same place: Manhattan, a **borough** in New York City. Transportation, tourist, and satellite maps each contain different information.

Think about your own town or region. If you were to create a map, what approach would you take? Would a map showing someone how to get from your home to your school be different from a map showing the location of places such as shopping malls and parks?

Try drawing your own map of the area around your home. Only include information that is important to you. Compare your map to an online map of the same area. How do your maps differ? How are they the same? Did you decide to leave anything out of your map?

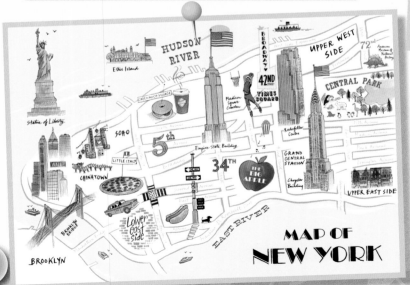

These maps are the official subway map of New York City (above) and a tourist map of Lower Manhattan (left). Which do you think would be more useful for a visitor to the city?

These maps are a 3D Google Earth map of Manhattan (above), a map of its streets and neighborhoods (below), and a hand-drawn map of its neighborhoods and attractions (left).

MORNINGSIDE HEIGHTS
Columbia University,
Grant's Tomb, Cathedral of
St. John the Devine

HARLEM Appolo Theatre,
The Studio Museum in Harlem,
The Shomberg Center for Research
in Black Culture

UPPER EAST SIDE
Guggenheim Museum,
Metropolitan Museum
of Art
Whitney Art Musem,
Central Park

UPPER WEST SIDE
Lincoln Centre, Columbus Ave,
Amsterdam Ave, Broadway,
Dakota Apartments,
The Dairy,
The Sheep Meadow,
Strawberry Field

MIDTOWN
Time Square,
Rockefeller Centre,
Chrysler Building,
Trump Tower, Broadway

MIDTOWN
Empire State Building,
St. Patricks Cathedral,
N.Y. Public Library,
Bryant Park

CHELSEA
Meatpacking District,
The High Line,
Chelsea Market

SOHO
Orchard Street,
Lower East Side,
Little Singer Building

GREENWICH VILLAGE
Washington Square,
Astor Place, Tribeca

CHINA TOWN
Little Italy, Civic Centre,
Nolita

LOWER MANHATTAN
Trinity Church, Wall Street,
New York Stock Exchange,
Bowling Green, World Financial Centre

Glossary

abstract Describes something that uses ideas or assumptions

astrolabe A device for measuring the height of stars above the horizon

astronomical Relating to space and heavenly bodies such as stars

bearing The direction of movement, expressed in degrees on a compass

borough A district of a city with its own government

cartogram A map which is distorted to show statistical information

cartographers People who draw and study maps

colonies Areas governed by a country in other parts of the world

compass A device with a needle that points toward the north

compass rose A circle on a map that shows bearing lines

computational geometry A branch of computer science that expresses information in terms of shapes

concentric A shape drawn inside another shape with the same outline

concrete Describes something that has measured, observable evidence

cosmological Related to a religious view of the universe

dataset A collection of related sets of information used by a computer

diameter The distance from side to side across a circle

digital Computerized

Geographic Information Systems Computer programs that use a wide range of sources to generate maps

geometric Having regular shapes

key An explanation of symbols and other information included on a map

Indigenous The original inhabitants of a specific geographic area and their descendants

media Different materials that can be used to create something

navigation Planning and following a journey by using a map

nervous system The network of cells and fibers that transmit nerve impulses around the body

oriented Adjusted to a particular surrounding

pilgrims People who travel to a sacred place for religious reasons

projection A way of representing a solid object on a flat surface

propaganda Material intended to persuade people to believe a particular point of view

radar A device for locating objects using radio signals

resolution The smallest detail visible in a photograph

satellite A spacecraft in orbit around Earth

scripture The holy books of a religion

sextant A device for measuring the height of stars above the horizon

spatial analysis The study of geographical data

spherical Shaped like a ball

statistical Based on numerical data

surveying The careful measurement and recording of details about land

tablets Flat clay slabs used for writing on in ancient times

taxation The process of raising money for government by charging citizens

thermal imaging The creation of pictures that show the presence of heat, or its absence

Western A set of ideals with origins in the traditional customs, beliefs, and heritage of western Europe

On the Web

www.nationalgeographic.com/ kids-world-atlas/maps.html
A National Geographic page with free downloadable maps of many parts of the world.

academic.emporia.edu/aberjame/ map/h_map/h_map.htm
A detailed account of the history of cartography, with links to key maps.

https://mrgris.com/projects/ merc-extreme/
An interactive site to explore the distortions of the Mercator Projection. Warps maps in real-time.

www.esa.int/esaKIDSen/ SEM5C6BE8JG_LifeinSpace_0.html
A page from the European Space Agency about the Hubble Space Telescope and its role in mapping the universe.

Books

Besel, Jennifer M. *What Is a Map?* Maps. Capstone Press, 2013.

Gillett, Jack, and Meg Gillett. *Transportation-Network Maps*. Maps of the Environmental World. PowerKids Press, 2012.

Hirsch, Rebecca E. *Using Climate Maps*. What Do You Know About Maps? Lerner Publications, 2016.

Hoe, Susan C. *Where We Live*. Maps and Mapping. Gareth Stevens Publishing, 2008.

Matteson, Adrienne. *Using Digital Maps*. Cherry Lake Publishing, 2013.

Somervill, Barbara A. *The Story Behind Maps*. True Stories. Heinemann, 2012.

Index